KATE RIGGS

grow with me

SUNFLOWER

CREATIVE EDUCATION

Published by Creative Education
P.O. Box 227, Mankato, Minnesota 56002
Creative Education is an imprint of
The Creative Company
www.thecreativecompany.us

Design and production by Ellen Huber
Art direction by Rita Marshall
Printed in the United States of America

Photographs by 123rf (Annie Desaulniers, Le Do),
Alamy (IMAGEMORE Co., Ltd.), Biosphoto (Carol
Sharp/Flowerphotos), Dreamstime (Elena Elisseeva,
Garsya, Haraldmuc, Karelgallas, Kornilovdream,
Oleksandr Kostiuchenko, Anette Linnea Rasmussen,
Filipe Varela), Getty Images (Maxine Adcock, Steve
Satushek, Pete Turner), iStockphoto (ansonsaw),
Science Photo Library (MAXINE ADCOCK, NIGEL
CATTLIN), Shutterstock (Garsya, Hasloo Group
Production Studio, haveseen, Tischenko Irina, jocic,
Evgen Kuzmin, Aga_Rafi, Dr. Ajay Kumar Singh,
TFoxFoto, P.Uzunova, Filipe B. Varela), Superstock
(Imagebroker.net), Veer (Kenneth Keifer, Justin Kral,
sad, Jan Skwara)

Library of Congress Cataloging-in-Publication Data
Riggs, Kate.
Sunflower / Kate Riggs.
p. cm. — (Grow with me)
Includes bibliographical references and index.
Summary: An exploration of the life cycle and
life span of sunflowers, using up-close photographs
and step-by-step text to follow a sunflower's growth
process from seed to seedling to mature plant.

ISBN 978-1-60818-218-3
1. Sunflowers—Life cycles—Juvenile literature.
2. Sunflowers—Seeds—Juvenile literature. I. Title.
SB299.S9R54 2012
635.9'3399—dc23   2011040501

First Edition
9 8 7 6 5 4 3 2 1

TABLE OF CONTENTS

4 *Sunflowers can go from 1 inch (2.5 cm) to 6 feet (1.8 m) tall in about 3 months.*

Sunflowers are annual plants. Annuals are plants that live for a year or less. They grow from seeds. Sunflowers grow best in **fertile** soil that gets plenty of water. They need bright sunlight, too.

Sunflowers are **native** to North and South America. Sunflowers are tall plants that can be 3 to 15 feet (0.9–4.6 m) high. Their wide, green leaves are 3 to 12 inches (7.6–30.5 cm) long.

5

6 *A sunflower head has 1,000 to 2,000 ray and disk flowers.*

A sunflower produces hundreds of seeds. The seeds are found in the flower head. The sunflower has two kinds of petals on the flower head. The disk flowers are in the middle of the head. They are usually brown. The yellow ray flowers grow around the disk flowers.

The seed is the beginning of a sunflower. It starts in the flower head, then it falls to the ground. The seed can stay on the ground for a long time. When the soil temperature reaches 40 to 50 °F (4.4 to 10 °C), the seed starts to **germinate** (*JER-mih-nate*).

7

The kernel inside the hull is the part of the sunflower seed that is eaten.

8 Seeds need water, light, and air to grow. A seed is dry. Inside the seed is an **embryo** (*EM-bree-oh*). The embryo is wrapped in a hard shell called a seed coat. Water softens the seed coat. Then the embryo gets bigger and breaks through the seed coat.

The seed's root grows down into the soil. Its seed coat comes off, and the first leaves appear. This plant is called a seedling.

The first root that grows out of the embryo is called the radicle.

9

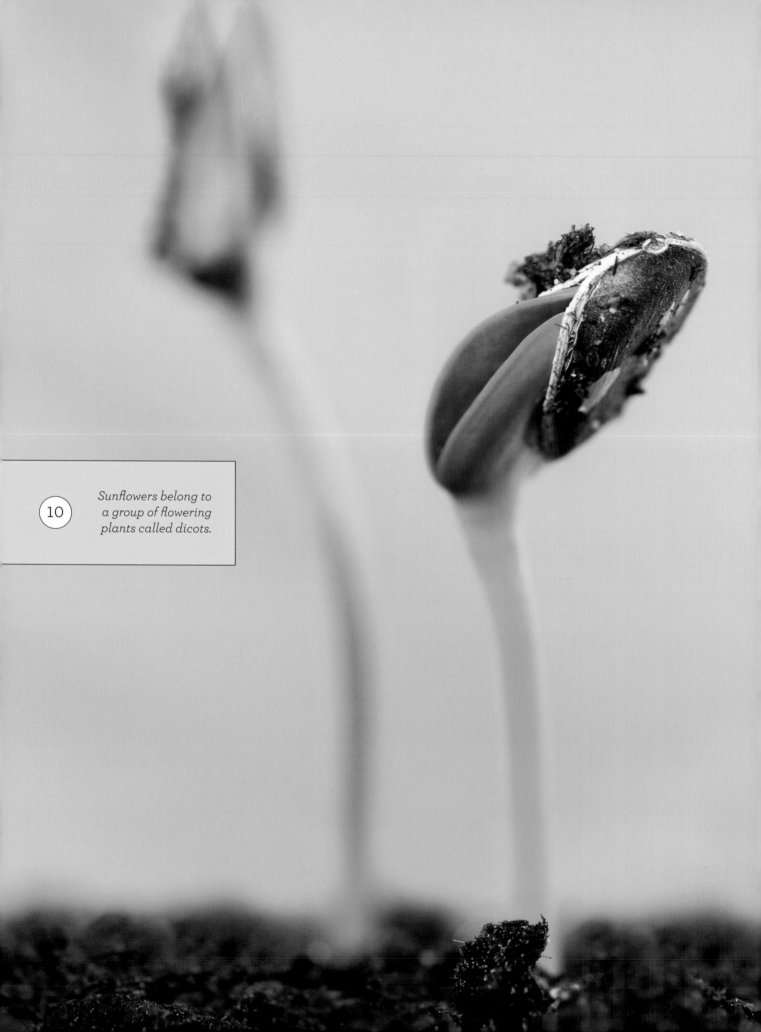

Sunflowers belong to a group of flowering plants called dicots.

Sunlight gives the seedling energy. Sunflowers need six to eight hours of sunlight each day. Air helps the seedling produce more energy to keep growing. A seedling uses sunlight, air, and water to make food for itself.

A seedling has three parts. The root is the first part. Then the shoot grows up out of the soil. The leaves branch off from the shoot. Sunflower seedlings have leaves in pairs.

11

Three days after it sprouts, a sunflower seedling may still have the seed coat hanging on. The coat falls away as the leaves open up. Seedlings grow quickly. They can grow more than one inch (2.5 cm) in a day.

After about 10 days, there are many leaves on the seedling. The leaves have tiny hairs on them. The leaves feel like sandpaper. The plant grows straight up into the air.

12

The hairs on a sunflower seedling make the leaves look fuzzy.

Sunflowers have deep roots. Some roots go down nine feet (2.7 m).

13

14 *This sunflower bud is getting bigger and is almost ready to bloom.*

A seedling becomes a young sunflower when it is one to two feet (30.5–61 cm) tall. It keeps growing, and a small bud forms. The bud is at the tip of the sunflower's stem. Between days 35 and 65, the bud develops.

The sunflower bud follows the path of the sun. It moves to face the sun wherever the sun is in the sky. It does this to get as much light as possible. In 6 to 12 weeks, the plant is fully grown. It stops following the sun.

15

Bees get liquid food called nectar from flowering plants such as sunflowers.

When the bud opens, the ray flowers spread out. At the center of the ray flowers are the disk flowers. The sunflower keeps blooming for at least another month. By 80 to 90 days after germination, the sunflower is completely flowering.

16

Insects such as bees like sunflowers. They go from flower to flower and pick up **pollen** on their legs. When bees land on disk flowers, they **pollinate** them. The disk flowers turn into seeds. They get harder, and seed coats cover them. Most sunflower shells are tan with dark stripes. Others are black.

The sunflower is the national flower of Russia and the state flower of Kansas.

Once the sunflowers are pollinated, the ray flowers shrivel up. Then the petals drop away. All that is left is the seed head.

The seed head is heavy. It makes the sunflower droop and point toward the ground. Birds like to eat sunflower seeds. They fly by and pick them out of the seed head.

18

Small birds perch, or land, on sunflower seed heads to pick out the seeds.

The stem of the plant is still green when the seed head starts to droop.

19

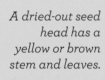

20

A dried-out seed head has a yellow or brown stem and leaves.

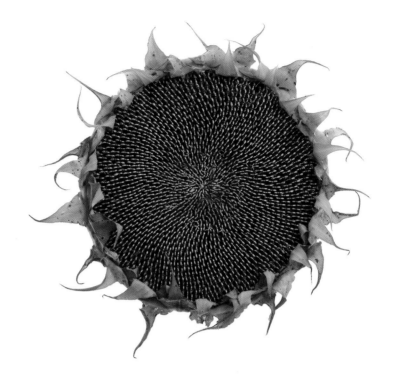

The seed head dries out at the end of summer.
The seeds fall to the ground. Some are
carried away by the wind. Animals eat many
other seeds.

The back of the seed head turns yellow. The
sunflower stem gets yellow, too. The leaves
wither and die. The seeds on the ground lie
dormant during the fall and winter.

People collect sunflower seeds to use them for many things. Many seeds are salted, roasted, and sold as snack foods. Others are fed to birds and **livestock**.

Sunflower seeds with black seed coats are full of oil. The seeds are crushed to release the oil. People use the oil for cooking and salad dressings. Some sunflower oil is used to make soap.

22

Sunflower oil can be stored in bottles or other containers.

Birds such as cardinals like eating black-oil sunflower seeds from feeders.

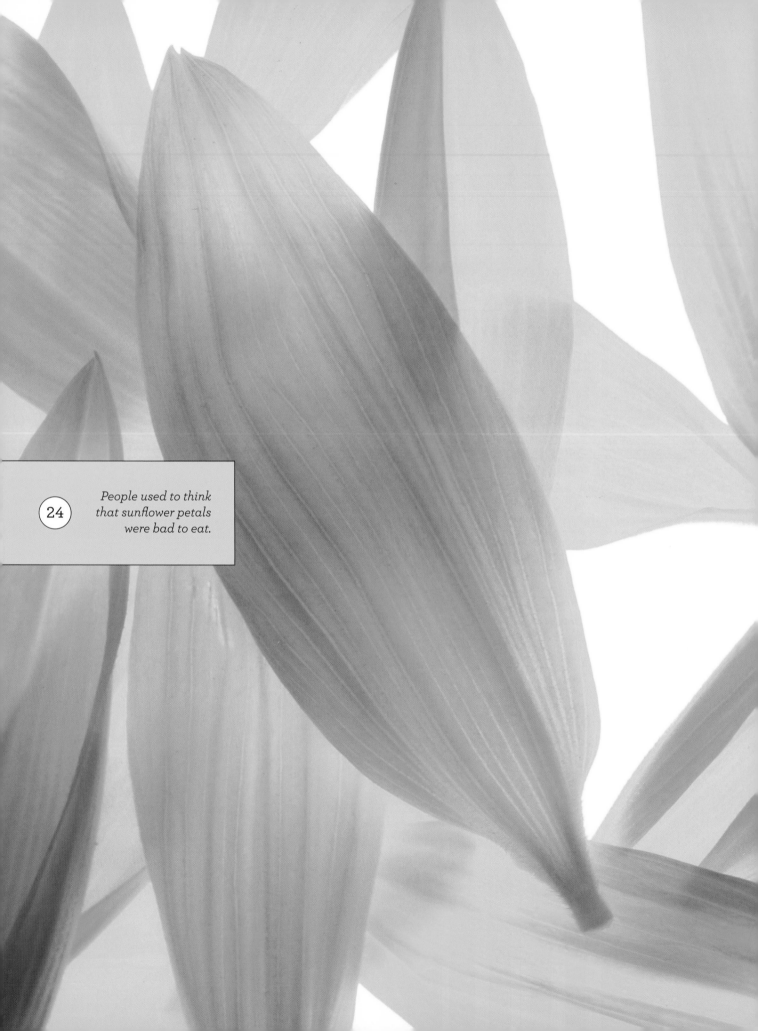

24 *People used to think that sunflower petals were bad to eat.*

26 feet

Some people cook sunflower petals as food. The petals can be made into a yellow dye, too. Long ago, people used the dye to turn clothes yellow.

People started growing sunflowers about 3,000 years ago. They found out that they could use the petals, seeds, and oil. They liked that the plants grew quickly and easily.

25

The tallest sunflower on record was almost 26 feet (7.9 m) high!

People still grow sunflowers. They plant them in fields and in gardens. Sometimes they first plant seeds in pots. The seeds need a sunny place to grow and a lot of water.

The seed begins to sprout. Soon it is a seedling. When the sunflower gets too big for the pot, it is planted in the warm ground.

26

There are more than 50 different species, or groups, of sunflower in the world.

These seedlings are in pots that can be planted in the ground.

27

When the small disk flowers dry out, they leave the seeds behind.

28 Sunflowers bloom until the soil gets too dry or until the first **frost**. They do not last through the winter. The same sunflower will not come back the following spring. A seed that takes root in the soil will turn into a new plant. It will sprout leaves and make seeds of its own. A new sunflower will greet the sun.

Sunflower plants grown in fields are left there over the winter.

29

A seed falls to the ground from a sunflower seed head.

The seed begins to germinate late in the spring.

The roots and leaves of a seedling appear.

The seedling grows for about 12 to 20 days.

30

At 1 to 2 feet (30.5–61 cm) tall, the plant is a young sunflower.

After 15 or more days, a bud forms on the sunflower.

The sunflower bud follows the sun until it flowers.

 The sunflower is pollinated, and seeds form.

The seed head dries out, and the plant dies.

dormant: *alive but not growing*

embryo: *the part of a seed that grows into a plant*

fertile: *able to help things grow*

frost: *a time of colder weather when ice forms and plants stop growing*

germinate: *start to grow*

insects: *animals that have six legs and one or two pairs of wings*

livestock: *farm animals such as chickens and cows*

native: *from a certain place*

pollen: *a yellow powder made by flowers that is used to fertilize other flowers*

pollinate: *take pollen from one flower to another to fertilize the plant, causing seeds to grow*

WEB SITES

DLTK's Sunflower Crafts for Kids
http://www.dltk-holidays.com/fall/crafts-sunflowers.htm
Make a sunflower mask or use seeds to create a sunflower.

National Sunflower Association: Coloring Book
http://www.sunflowernsa.com/all-about/coloring-book/
Download a coloring book that is all about sunflowers.

READ MORE

Legg, Gerald. *From Seed to Sunflower.*
New York: Franklin Watts, 1998.

Schaefer, Lola. *This Is the Sunflower.*
New York: Greenwillow Books, 2000.

32

INDEX